ELIZABETH RING

Search and Rescue Dogs

EXPERT TRACKERS AND TRAILERS

GOOD DOGS!
THE MILLBROOK PRESS ▪ BROOKFIELD, CONNECTICUT

**FOR KENDEL:
RIGHT ON TRACK**

Cover photo courtesy of Bill Hennefrund
Photos courtesy of Photo Researchers: pp. 3, 23; Kent and
Donna Dannen: pp. 4, 12, 15; David and Hilda Onderdonk: p. 7;
Bettmann Archive: p. 9; Marian Hardy: pp. 11, 18, 26; Gerlinda
V. Hockla: p. 17; Vickie King: p. 20; Judy Graham: pp. 27, 28.

Library of Congress Cataloging-in-Publication Data
Ring, Elizabeth, 1920–
Search and rescue dogs : expert trackers and trailers
/ by Elizabeth Ring.
p.   cm. — (Good dogs!)
Includes bibliographical references (p.   ) and index.
Summary: Dogs of all breeds (and mixed breeds) can
be trained to be SAR dogs. This book describes these
nose-to-the-ground rescue workers and the organizations
that direct their work.
ISBN 1-56294-294-8 (lib. bdg.)
1. Search dogs—Juvenile literature.   2. Rescue dogs—Juvenile
literature.   3. Search and rescue operations—Juvenile literature.
[1. Search dogs.   2. Rescue dogs.   3. Rescue work.]   I. Title.
II. Series: Ring, Elizabeth, 1920–   Good dogs!
SF428.73.R56   1994
636.7′0886—dc20   93-42278   CIP   AC

Published by The Millbrook Press
2 Old New Milford Road
Brookfield, Connecticut 06804

SEARCH AND RESCUE DOGS

The bloodhound may be the oldest breed of hound that hunts by scent. It is an ideal dog for tracking and search and rescue.

Alex Ellis had never visited the country before. Never been in upstate New York. Never been near a farm. It was all very different from the city.

But Alex liked Mr. and Mrs. Beals, old friends of his parents. He liked Trish and Hank, the Beals kids, too. This could be the best couple of weeks he had spent in all his eight years.

But that very afternoon things started to go wrong. The Bealses' calico cat scratched him. The horse tossed its head and neighed when Alex climbed over a fence. Then, late that night, the eerie screech of an owl nearly scared him right out of his bed. Toward morning a couple of raccoons got into a screaming fight right under his window.

Alex went to breakfast feeling shaky and cross. He didn't complain to the Bealses. He simply decided country life was not for him and he was going to walk home — right down the country road and back to the city.

When everybody was busy with chores, Alex left. He walked and walked. The sun got high and hot, and he got tired and thirsty. When he saw an empty farm truck out in a field, he climbed into the front seat to rest. He fell sound asleep.

Back at the farm, the Bealses were looking all over for Alex. When they could not find him in the house or the barn or the woods nearby, they panicked. They called the local sheriff to ask if he could help out.

''Sure,'' said the sheriff, ''and we'll get the Rensselear

County Search and Rescue Team and the Onderdonks' blood-hounds on the search. That will be the quickest, surest way to find the boy. I'll give the Onderdonks a call. David and Hilda are always ready for an emergency.''

Before long, the sheriff and David Onderdonk arrived at the farm. Out of the backseat of the car plopped Martini, a floppy-eared, wrinkle-browed bloodhound. Martini took a whiff of Alex's pajamas.

David said ''Find him!'' and the dog started sniffing for the boy's trail. When she hit on it, she pulled hard on her long leash. She yanked David out the gate and down the road, trotting hard on the trail. They had gone a good way when Martini swerved off the road toward the farm truck parked in the field. Alex, sound asleep in the truck, woke up to find Martini licking his face all over.

''Yow!'' he yelled. He was sure he was being eaten alive.

''Down!'' David quickly told the dog. He caught Alex up in his arms. He told Alex how Martini was just saying, ''Hi, Sport. Glad I found you.''

Back at the farm again, Alex explained about being scared and homesick. Everybody was sorry, but they all thought he would like the country once he got used to it. Alex was not so sure. He sat down on the top step of the porch to think things over.

Just then Martini came over and flopped down beside him. She rested her head against Alex's leg and looked up, like a sor-rowful clown, into Alex's face. It wasn't long before Alex de-cided to stay at the farm.

Martini, out of harness after a successful search and
rescue mission, returns home with David Onderdonk.

This was just one of the dozens of times the Onderdonks' bloodhounds had found someone who was lost or in hiding or running away. The Rensselaer County Search and Rescue Team had been famous for their work for a long time.

THE STORY OF SEARCH AND RESCUE DOGS ▪ There are many kinds of search and rescue dogs, and Martini belongs to one of the oldest breeds. The bloodhound's European ancestors were said to be great trailers in the A.D. 700s.

Since the early eighteenth century (and possibly earlier) in the Swiss Alps, Saint Bernards have helped rescue people lost in blizzards or buried by avalanches.

In the United States, search-dog history goes back to colonial days. Many dogs (of many breeds) were trained to track people—not always to "rescue" them but more often to catch a trespasser or a thief.

Today, search and rescue (SAR) dog teams go on many "mercy runs." They search for children, campers, hikers, and other people who have lost their way. They also search for people who have been trapped by avalanches, floods, earthquakes, volcanoes, fires, plane crashes, train wrecks, and other disasters. SAR dogs can do the job of twenty to thirty people—faster and surer.

SAR organizations have been active in the United States and Canada since the early 1960s, and more groups are forming every year. Large national groups include the National Associa-

In this historical print, a Saint Bernard finds an avalanche victim partially buried in the snow. The dog alerts rescuers, who know that its barking means, "Help! Help! Come save someone!"

tion for Search and Rescue (NASAR), the American Rescue Dog Association (ARDA), and the National Police Bloodhound Association (NPBA). Other organizations, such as Dogs East, serve specific regions of the country.

Each SAR unit has its own way of working. Most SAR people are volunteers — teachers, nurses, homemakers, business owners, and people in other occupations. Some organizations work locally. Like the Onderdonks, they help sheriffs, park rangers, and other officials who may or may not have search dogs of their own. Larger organizations, such as NASAR, are made up of many independent SAR dog units that can go wherever help is needed. Sometimes teams need air transportation to take them to distant or hard-to-reach places.

American SAR organizations have also joined foreign search groups in rescue operations in other countries. In 1985, for instance, American SAR dogs were flown to Mexico City to search for victims of a devastating earthquake. Dogs from France and Switzerland were there also.

CHARACTERISTICS OF SAR DOGS ▪ An SAR dog is intelligent, calm, and steady. (No chasing after a rabbit that crosses its path!) It is friendly and adaptable. It can work in unusual circumstances in unfamiliar places among strange people. And it is strong and healthy.

Most important to SAR work is a dog's sense of smell. All dogs are born with keen scenting abilities. We do not yet understand exactly how dogs can smell as well as they do, but scientists have made some good guesses.

A dog has about 220 million scent cells spread over the many folds in the lining of its nose. (A human nose has only about 5 million scent cells.) If you could stretch out the lining of

A rescue worker and dog search through a collapsed
building in Mexico City after the 1985 earthquake.

a dog's nose in a flat sheet, the lining would be larger than the
surface of the dog's entire body! That is one good reason why a
dog's sense of smell is a million or more times better than ours
—depending on the strength of the scent.

Hilda Onderdonk explains how ground-scenting dogs like
Martini follow a trail:

A German shepherd keeps its nose to the ground in
a search for a missing child. The handler nearest the dog
holds a strip of cloth in the air to test wind direction.

"Pull out the front of your shirt," Hilda says. "Do you feel hot air rising? Your body heats the air around you. That hot air rises, bringing up bits of skin and the bacteria that feed on them. Your body is constantly shedding skin cells—50 to 60 million every day. The bits of skin, called rafts, rise from your body, cool off, and fall. It's like an umbrella of invisible dandruff as the rafts drift down around your feet. If the rafts blow off in a breeze, they settle in the bushes and grass. These are the scent patterns a bloodhound trails."

It is easiest for a dog to follow a trail on a calm, cool, damp day, when the ground is a bit warmer than the air—as in the fall. On a day like that, scent clings to the ground.

Some SAR dogs are primarily "ground scenters," tracking a scent on the ground. Others are "air scenters." Most can do both but are better at one kind of scenting than the other.

Dogs use their other senses too, of course—sight, hearing, touch, and taste—to tell what is around them and where they are going. But it is mostly their well-trained scenting ability that makes them so successful at their jobs.

DOGS IN SAR WORK ▪ Dogs of all breeds (and mixed breeds) can be trained to be SAR dogs. Some breeds (such as bloodhounds and German shepherds) are champs at covering miles of rough country; others (such as malamutes and Saint Bernards) are famous for their work in ice and snow. Still others (such as Newfoundlands and Labrador retrievers) are completely at home in the water.

Bloodhounds are known as the "kings (and queens) of trailing hounds." A bloodhound, it is said, "can't see beans in a pan, but it can smell a bean a mile away." This powerful black-and-tan (sometimes reddish) dog is a masterful ground scenter. It tracks like a locomotive, snuffling along, picking up scent from the bushes or ground. It is hard to pull a bloodhound off a trail it is on.

No one knows just why bloodhounds are called "bloodhounds." In spite of tales about their "vicious, man-eating" ways, their name does *not* mean that they are "bloodthirsty." They are the gentlest of dogs — generous, like Martini, with their slobbery kisses.

Saint Bernards are big, gentle, bearlike dogs. In spite of their sad eyes and droopy jowls, they are playful and affectionate. They love snow and are thick-coated enough to stay warm in extreme cold. Their big strong feet carry them over icy slopes and their close-set toes help them "swim" through deep, soft drifts.

Saint Bernards use their keen air-scenting ability to locate people. They can detect human scent from several miles away. Even when people are buried 6 to 10 feet (almost 2 to 3 meters) deep in snow, scent from their warm bodies rises to the snow's surface and into the air — at least for a short time.

In the Swiss Alps in the sixteenth century, Saint Bernards were trained by monks at a monastery founded by Saint Bernard de Menthon in the late tenth century as a travelers' refuge. The dogs helped the monks patrol a treacherous mountain pass between Switzerland and Italy. The teams saved many travelers

A handler puts a bloodhound through a practice tracking course.

lost in storms and avalanches. The most famous of these dogs was a hero named Barry. In his twelve years of rescue work he saved about forty people.

Today, cars, highways, and tunnels make mountain travel much safer. Helicopters are often used in mountain rescues, and lighter-weight SAR dogs, such as 80-pound (32-kilogram) German shepherds, have for the most part replaced the 160-pound (73-kilogram) Saint Bernards. Even so, in the Colorado mountains, as well as in the Swiss Alps, Saint Bernards are still sometimes used to rescue a trapped hiker or skier.

Newfoundlands are the champions of water rescues. As big —150 pounds (68 kilograms)—gentle, and bearlike as a Saint Bernard, the ''Newf'' loves the water. Over the years, a strong rescue instinct has been bred into the dog. Newfs sometimes even insist on saving swimmers who do not need to be saved.

The close-set toes on the feet of the Newfoundland make the dog a powerful swimmer, even in huge waves. It can dive and swim underwater. It does not ''dog paddle'' as most dogs do, but swims with strong breaststrokes. The Newf's dense oily coat keeps it warm and sheds water. The ears lie close to the body, which helps keep water out, and the strong muscled tail acts as a rudder. The dog's great strength and stamina make it able to cope with rough seas.

Most Newfs are coal black, but some are black and white, called ''Landseers'' for Sir Edwin Landseer, a British artist. Landseer's painting of a two-color Newf made the dog very popular in nineteenth-century England.

The Newfoundland's dense oily coat is only one of the qualities that makes it a valuable water-rescue dog. The Newf is also an unbelievably powerful swimmer with a natural rescue instinct.

The Newf comes from the province of Newfoundland in Canada. Natural retrievers, the dogs were once fishermen's helpers. Many were ship's dogs—used as living life preservers at sea. They would also jump into the sea and pull nets full of fish up to the boats. Newfs have saved hundreds of lives at sea by carrying lifelines to sinking boats and rescuing people from the water.

In the United States today, Newfoundlands are chiefly companion and guard dogs. Some, however, are trained to rescue people in water, woodlands, and snow.

German shepherds are great all-around working dogs. These highly intelligent dogs are strong, agile, courageous, and easy to train. They are tops in police service as patrol dogs and detector

German shepherds are very popular for search and rescue work. Here a dog and two trackers trail a scent in Shenandoah National Park in Virginia.

dogs. In military service, their keen senses of hearing and smell make them alert guards. They also work as guide dogs for blind people. As search and rescue dogs, they are matchless in their ability to locate a person's scent in the air. They have strong ground-scenting skills too.

German shepherds take part in rescue efforts all over the world. They work with the Avalanche Search program in mountainous parts of France, Switzerland, Austria, and Italy. In 1980, ARDA's all-German shepherd teams were on duty after Mount St. Helens erupted in Washington state.

Other breeds that serve as SAR dogs include Labrador and golden retrievers, airedales, collies, beagles, standard schnauzers, Irish setters, rottweilers, mastiffs, Doberman pinschers, malamutes, and mixed breeds.

SAR TEAMS AT WORK ▪ The people in each SAR unit are well trained for emergencies. SAR members are athletic. They like camping, hiking, mountain climbing (or skiing, boating, or diving, depending on where they live). They are trained in map reading and survival techniques. They know how to give first-aid treatments to victims, to themselves, and to their dogs. Above all, they love their dogs—their working partners and friends —and know how to train them, tend them, and ''read'' their behavior on a trail.

Wilderness Rescue. Late one night in Hooper, Utah, Vickie King got a call from the local sheriff. A member of American

Vickie King's golden retriever McKenna pauses during a cave search.
The headlamp helps both the dog and the human rescuers to see.

Search Dogs Inc., Vickie and her golden retriever, McKenna, wasted no time hitting the road to help find a lost hiker.

A Utah Civil Air Patrol airplane carried Vickie and McKenna and three other SAR teams into the mountains. Each team was assigned an area to cover.

On the ground, Vickie let McKenna sniff a handkerchief that belonged to Linda, the lost hiker. Then they set off. Together they climbed over rocks, plunged through woods, and came close to falling off a cliff. They searched for hours, keeping in touch with the other teams by radio. By late afternoon, the SAR teams had cut the search area from many square miles to less than half a square mile (1.3 square kilometers). The airplane pilot, alerted by radio, circled that area and spotted the lost hiker on a rock in the woods.

Hungry and thirsty, Linda was airlifted out of the wilderness —but not before she had met all the dogs that had spent the day zeroing in on her location. For the dogs, it was important to meet the person they had searched for—to give them a sense of a mission accomplished. They *all* took Linda's thanks and praise as their rightful reward.

Wilderness-Search Training. Ground-search training includes practice in tracking, trailing, and air scenting. In tracking, a dog learns to follow the person's footsteps. In trailing, a dog is taught to follow scents that may have drifted some distance from the actual track. In air scenting, a dog is trained to sniff the air for a particular human scent. Most SAR dogs are first trained to air scent.

In one lesson, a trail layer (not the dog's handler, who is always behind the dog, never ahead) makes short, straight tracks for the dog to follow, then longer trails that turn this way and that. After a while, the dog learns to ''cast,'' circling and sniffing to pick up the trail of the layer's scent. Within a month or two, a dog can follow a trail as long as a half mile (1.3 kilometers).

The lessons get longer and harder. Two or three people lay tracks that crisscross confusingly. Trail layers climb trees, hide behind stone walls, and test the dog in other tricky ways.

For eighteen months to two years, dogs are trained on all kinds of terrain and in all kinds of weather. They practice riding in cars, trains, boats, ski lifts, and trams. Some are carefully lowered (in special harnesses) from cliff tops and helicopters. After hours of slow, patient work, dogs are taught to search for any human smell anywhere. And practicing continues even after they are working SAR dogs. In fact, training—for both dog and handler—never ends.

Snow Rescue. One March day in 1982 an avalanche swooped down on the Alpine Meadows Ski Area in California. The WOOF Search Dog Unit was called to the scene. Before long, seven bodies were found. But after five days, some skiers were still missing. Nobody had high hopes of finding anyone alive.

Then, at one spot on the mountainside, a German shepherd named Bridget stopped and barked. She pawed at the snow under her feet. Roberta Huber, Bridget's handler, and others started to dig—5 feet (1.5 meters), 7 feet (2 meters) down. Had Bridget made a mistake?

At that point they heard a faint, muffled voice: "I'm okay! I'm alive!"

When they reached Anna Conrad, she was huddled in blankets in an airspace under part of a building that had been almost crushed by the avalanche. After Anna was pulled out, the dog

Avalanches are common in the mountains of France. Here a German shepherd and rescue workers dig in the snow to search for buried skiers.

grabbed a piece of wood and tossed it into the air, over and over. It looked to everyone there as if Bridget was celebrating.

Snow-search training teaches dogs to search for human scent percolating up through the snow and to pay attention to the faint sounds dogs can hear much better than people.

Training often begins with the dog searching for its trainer hidden in snow. Then the dog practices searching for strangers.

In time, the dog finds pretend victims buried in deep trenches and snow caves.

Saint Bernards were once trained to work in teams of two or four dogs. When a victim was found, one dog (or two) would lie down to warm the person; the other dog (or two) would run for help. In spite of what you sometimes see in pictures, they never carried casks of brandy around their necks.

Water Rescue. One cold December day in New England, Gerlinde Hockla, an expert dog handler, was out walking seven dogs (three Newfoundlands, three Labrador retrievers, and a pointer) around a half-frozen pond.

Only one Newfoundland, Gus (an older dog with a habit of running off), was on leash. The others roamed free. Boomer, a young, bouncy Newf, took it into his head to run out on the ice. When he reached the middle of the pond, the ice broke. Boomer howled and splashed frantically, unable to get a grip on the edge of the ice. (As it turned out later, he had hurt his rear leg when he fell in.)

Suddenly, Gus pulled his leash out of Gerlinde's hand and galloped toward Boomer. Just as he reached the thrashing dog, he too fell in.

As Boomer continued to howl helplessly, Gus started breaking a path through the ice toward shore. Time after time, he rose out of the water and threw his weight down on the ice — just like a sledgehammer. When he reached shore, he swam back to

Boomer and, after many tries, he got Boomer to follow him to dry land.

That winter, the pond froze and refroze several times, but Gus's lifesaving path through the ice remained visible for months. No wonder the Newfoundland Club of America gave him its ''hero'' award that year!

Nobody had trained Gus to do what he did. He seemed to act partly out of that inbred Newfoundland instinct—to save a creature in danger of drowning—and (in breaking the path) partly out of self-preservation. However, there are training programs for water-rescue work, and not only Newfs but Labrador retrievers, German shepherds, and other breeds take part.

Water-search training often starts with water games such as fetching a ball or a stick. Then the dog is encouraged to swim out to where a handler is treading water. The game gradually moves farther from shore into deeper water. In endurance training the dog swims 4 miles (6 kilometers) or more in open ocean.

In an exercise in locating someone who has sunk or drowned, a diver dives as deep as 30 feet (10 meters). The dog swims out to the area or is taken out in a boat. It is taught to signal (by circling, whining, or putting its nose to the water) when it detects the diver's scent. In shallow water, the dog dives down and tries to pull up the ''victim'' and drag him to shore. Sometimes, the dog makes its search from shore and either signals or swims out to the site.

A schnauzer searches for a drowning victim in the New River in Virginia. The handlers stand by to assist the dog.

In advanced water-rescue training, a dog is taught to leap from a boat and carry a lightweight rope in its mouth to shore. It also learns to tow people by grabbing their clothes with its teeth. Sometimes two dogs work together, one on each side of a person so the person can hold onto both dogs to be towed to safety.

Disaster Rescue. In Armenia, in 1988, a terrible earthquake killed many people. Children were lost. Families were separated.

International search and rescue operations started almost immediately. From the United States, eight SAR teams (six women and two men with five German shepherds, two Newfoundlands, a rottweiler, and a golden retriever) were flown overseas.

A rescue worker follows the dog's lead as it searches for any evidence of human life under the rubble at a disaster site.

A search and rescue dog's job is very difficult and sometimes dangerous. This German shepherd appears to have earned a rest.

In ten days of constant noise and confusion, the dogs searched the rubble, hardly resting. In the end, many people were rescued and many bodies were found. The survivors, of course, will never forget the terrible earthquake, but they will also always remember the dogs that helped save them from being buried alive.

Disaster-search training is not very different from ground-search training. But it does teach dogs to find human scent under rocks, earth, twisted lumber and metal, and other rubble caused by disasters. Teams must often work in the dark or under blinding searchlights. Unlike wilderness searches, workers carry little equipment other than flashlights or the radios that keep them in touch with each other and with team leaders.

Dogs are trained off leash to pick their way carefully over shaky piles of sharp debris. They often wear sturdy booties to protect their feet. When a dog finds someone (dead or alive), it might signal by wagging its tail and, with ears pointing forward, scratch at a spot. In a "body find," a dog often signals by flattening its ears and tucking its tail between its hind legs. Handlers are certain that some dogs know the difference between the living and dead.

Fortunately, search and rescue people get many more calls for rescue work than for body searches. SAR members—both persons and dogs—are always ready and eager to answer a call for help. What better service could a lost person (or relatives of a victim) wish for than an SAR team's expert assistance?

FURTHER READING

Caras, Roger. *Yankee: The Inside Story of a Champion Blood-hound.* New York: Putnam, 1979.

Emert, Phyllis. *Search and Rescue Dogs.* New York: Crestwood House, 1985.

Fichter, George. *Working Dogs.* New York: Watts, 1979.

Hart, Audrey and Edward Hart. *Working Dogs.* London: P. T. Batsford, 1984.

McCloy, James. *Dogs at Work.* New York: Crown, 1979.

Pope, Joyce. *Taking Care of Your Dog.* New York: Watts, 1990.

INDEX

Page numbers in *italics* refer to illustrations.

Airedales, 19
American Rescue Dog Association (ARDA), 9, 19
American Search Dogs Inc., 19–20
Armenia earthquake, 26–28
Avalanches, 8, *9,* 14, 16, 19, 22, *23*

Barry (Saint Bernard), 16
Beagles, 19
Bloodhounds, *4,* 6, *7,* 8, 13, 14, *15*
Boomer (Newfoundland), 24–25
Bridget (German shepherd), 22–23

Collies, 19

Conrad, Anna, 22

Disaster rescue, 8, 10, *11,* 26–29, *27*
Doberman pinschers, 19
Dogs East, 9

Earthquakes, 8, 10, *11,* 26–29
Ellis, Alex, 5–6

German shepherds, *12,* 13, 16, *18,* 18–19, *23,* 25, 27, *28*
Golden retrievers, 19, 27
Guide dogs, 19
Gus (Newfoundland), 24–25

Hockla, Gerlinde, 24
Huber, Roberta, 22

Irish setters, 19

King, Vickie, 19–21